THE KNOT GARDEN

THE KNOT GARDEN

poems by

Allison Funk

THE SHEEP MEADOW PRESS
RIVERDALE-ON-HUDSON, NEW YORK

All inquiries and permission requests should be addressed to:
The Sheep Meadow Press
PO Box 1345
Riverdale-on-Hudson, NY 10471

Cover: *Virginia Wolf* by Vanessa Bell
Photo of Allison Funk: David Funk

Designed and typeset by S.M.
Distributed by The University Press of New England.

Library of Congress Cataloguing-in-Publication Data

Funk, Allison.
    The knot garden: poems / by Allison Funk
        p. cm.
    ISBN 1-931357-06-4
        I. Title

PS3556.U62 K58 2002
811'.54--dc21

                                                                2002191180

We are grateful to the New York State Council on the Arts, a state agency, for their support.

The Sheep Meadow Press gratefully acknowledges a grant from the National Endowment for the Arts.

Acknowledgments

Grateful acknowledgment is made to the following journals in which these poems first appeared (sometimes in earlier versions and with different titles): *Crab Orchard Review*: "Trained, Wild or Translucent"; "The Seed of Her Name." *Delmar*: "Study for *Adam and Eve, 1913*"; "Untitled Drawing." *Drumvoices Revue*: "Late Summer, Cicadas." *Field*: "Florescence"; "Ruined." *Image: A Journal of the Arts and Religion*: "The Prodigal's Mother Speaks to God." *The Journal*: "Study for an Interior With the Artist, Leslie Stephen and Virginia Woolf"; "Landscape in Wartime, May 1941"; "The Storm." *River Styx*: "Self-Portrait of the Artist"; "The Artist in Her Studio"; "Study for *Interior With Two Women, 1932*." *The Paris Review*: "On Pruning." *Pleiades*: "How It Ends." *Poetry*: "Mount Joy"; "Memorial." *Shenandoah*: "Tallulah Falls"; "Heart's-ease"; "The Deer.." The sequence of poems, "From the Sketchbooks of Vanessa Bell," was previously published as a chapbook by Parallel Press, at the University of Wisconsin, Madison.

The opening epigraph for this book is from John Burnside's poem, "The Hay Devil," in *The Asylum Dance*, published by Jonathan Cape in London, 2000.

I wish to thank Southern Illinois University at Edwardsville for the generous faculty grants that supported the writing of these poems. I am also grateful to the Ragdale Foundation, where some of the poems in this book were written. I am deeply indebted to Jennifer Atkinson, John Burnside, Jeff Hamilton, Howard Levy, Cleopatra Mathis, Eric Pankey, Jason Sommer, Jane Wayne, and my husband, George Soule, for their abiding friendship and good advice.

for George

Contents

From the Sketchbooks of Vanessa Bell

In the Heartland

I never quite arrive

at absence

　　　which is presence somewhere else
in some bright field

　　　　some miracle of air.

John Burnside

On Pruning

On Pruning

Cut it way back.
Do not be afraid to pinch the first,
the only blossom. The berry cannot thrive
in freedom. Have no mercy,

gardener. Train the tree to a leader
crowned by the uppermost bud.
Make ten o'clock your angle
for the outstretched limbs
of the apple. Prune
when the knife is sharp,
taking care that the scar be neat.
To share the surgeon's belief in healing,
you must trust what has been taken from you
is a blessing. Trust

by April the cherry and pear
will fill in, stitching
the dreamiest lace, *punto in aria*,
think of it
as a veil if you must.

And the rose, this is a special case.
When winter's close, cut back
the tallest stems, then with soil
topped with straw or leaves, bury the plant,
make the mound as high as you can,
as if the grave were your own
impermanent home, as if you believed anything
could bloom again.

Afterimages

Where have they wintered,
the battered ones?
What compass guides them?

Questions she will ask,
though not until spring,
the girl in a Delaware autumn

who sees herself elsewhere,
shining in the plumage
and primaries of the Tropics.

Dazzled by the Monarchs
dressing the pin oak they've chosen
to roost in behind her house

she'd abandon everything
to follow them into another season
and so she makes her wish—

whither thou goest—
so strong is her longing
to blur off course,

migrate to another coast
to escape the snow that,
foiling her, will fall,

will cover her
in her winter land.
No matter,

she will console herself until spring,
when among last year's leaves
she'll look for a trace of topaz

and the telltale flashes
along the edge of a wing.
Who knows which among the venturing

return, even which generation
passes above shadows
of the girl, the tree

roosted in once? Afterimages,
the girl, the tree
familiar after this much time,

the headiness of flight,
the distance traveled from her,
the girl I come back to.

Poppy

Cover Girl's own
"coral red" or "hot poppy,"

a shade of cheap lipstick
I'd find in the bins at old Woolworth's:

a single flower
sets my yard on fire.

And in its light,
an adolescent takes hold of me,

through the gauzy years
pulls me down. Her face—

marked as the poppy's
by its purplish-brown stain—

in mine:
what I get

for being the only eleven-year-old in class
not to make fun of her birthmark

or the shock of white hair that falls
into her eyes. Snow in June, age

on youth, girls don't play like this, but my
get off

is useless, as muted
as the strains of my friends' voices at recess

swept from the dusty bases,
the four-square games,

swinging round, floating up.
Airborne.

All this time
the dark spot darkening—

as if drawn there,
at the heart of the flower

a star, and
beneath,

where the seeds
lie,

unable to breathe,
me.

Tallulah Falls

Tallulah. Three steps on the tongue.
As easy as falling.

It could be any wet rock,

over and over again
the milky explosions
of rhododendron,

a river
counting the ways

possible
to lose one's footing—

L'eau d'Or, Tempesta, Bridal Veil,

the beautiful seductions:

falling away, falling from,

none of them *failing.*

And yet she will not be dissuaded
it's legend

the rush
and stumble through gorge and mountains

lights up a city
somewhere,

too far away for her to see.

So—another rhythm—
not *huckleberry*.

Birthroot.
Wakerobin.

Let her flower be
the persistent trillium

native to this gorge.

And her crossing—

as skillful
as the Great Wallenda's

on any rope strung from one side
to another.

Surprise Lily

It's what we called in the sixties
"flesh colored,"
               thinking of no one's
but our own,
sure of our place in the world,
our modest
but always-to-be-counted-on homes.

Surprise. Surprise.

A lily's name.

     Or what she felt
one day long ago at the lake,

the girl who shot up
that summer, all stem,
budding as suddenly

as the top of her two-piece
came undone
without warning—

and from where it perched
rose above
the girl on the aquaplane
to wing beyond the green wake
she was riding.

At the same time
a cry went up—

> the way a bird seems sometimes
to carry a voice—
and the girl went under.

There would be a scar.

But the worst of it for her
(*imagine*)

wasn't that other blossoming
under water after she fell
and the board struck her, tearing her skin,

but coming up
the laughingstock
of a boat full of young men.

> *Naked lady*
we'll call this lily,
for her.

Innocence.

We've looked,
finding it nowhere else.

How It Ends

I'd trained for this,
holding my breath longer
and longer, becoming familiar

with the little chill just under the surface,
the muddy-yellow I'd call hazel
in someone looking back at me.

But the day I tried to cross the cove
under water I came to grips with nothing
I'd ever faced before.

Wrestling through fish lines,
a welter of weeds,
I fell to downy bottom

where somebody's dropped ski
lay next to the little rise of a life jacket,
a crosshatching of sunken oars.

Topographer, embellish this
with whatever you've been parted from—
oh my own loved ones, into this relief

I would come to rest,
a propeller spinning
slowly above me, my north star

amid the smaller clustered sunnies
chasing a shower of bait.
Then the firmament darkened

so quickly (I'm sorry—
I know you want to understand)
I cannot tell you how it ends.

in memory of FJF, 1945-1962

Sotto Voce

You know how fish
    can come across you swimming,
through a dusk
    you can't see
down past

brush your thigh.
    Maybe it's your warmth
they're after—the quick flush of it—
    though, betting,
you're more likely in the way,

shoal or depths
    the destination
of the fish, yours
    the arch
they're only passing through.

Was she thinking this
    when what might have been
the length of him
    (she couldn't see)
swish-swished her,

which was which—
    his current, water's,
the two washing sweetly
    against her together?
Oh, what was that song

still vaguely familiar?
    Only this she's clear on:

how they'd stripped to swim
     naked in the bay. Young,
unreasoning, the others farther out

and him she'd met that evening.
     She could hardly conjure
his face in the dark,
     though now it's coming back to her,
sotto voce, the undertow

that might have carried her away.
     Could have.
Unless she reached her hand down
     to divide them.
His, hers—

anyone's truth is soggy,
     a flood plain at worst.
What's the use of a levee
     or gate when the rain's
always falling?

From where she lives
     these many years later
she can see the fields by the river
     submerged. Dead center:
the axis of the tallest tree

she measures herself against,
     muddy water part way up,
the better half untouched,
     though the river is still rising,
hasn't reached its crest—what then

if she wasn't questioning
     her capacity for affection?

Sweet, sweet sap
    running underneath.
Had she never known passion?

At the Edge of the Woods

I should close her eyes. I want to,

but I can't move my hand to her face
where the short hairs look combed,
so neatly do they lean in one direction
the color of sand.

Along the road at the edge of the woods
where I spent my childhood
a deer
showing no sign of violence done to her,
no evidence she was shot or hit.

If not, how did she come to rest
in so formal an attitude,
why, when the woods we share
are so plentiful: leaves bark lichen moss—

at the creek behind my house
she could still be quenching her thirst.

Ovid wrote that some of us are changed just once
and live forever in that shape.

Others transform themselves at will.

Which am I? And the deer,

whom I half expect
to twitch
under the fly that has alighted
on a cheek's single brushstroke of blood,

I wonder if I may be inventing her
because I see everything living as wounded.

Heart's-ease

Heart's-ease

Weathervane heart spinning, horse and driver,
how will they get home, rain turning to ice
on the back roads of Indiana?

An itinerant preacher
traveling from one soul to the next. East,
west, fouled compass—

the tired horse lifts her feet
and the man tries to remember his God
that lately he's taken to calling

by the name of a flower
he's heard of.
Where does it blossom? he wonders,

far now from his children,
where they're sitting, he prays,
round the table saying the blessing.

Then Helen or Esther (whose turn *is* it tonight?)
will rise to recite from the Bible. Lord,
the words coming to mind, all

the Reverend can think of, back wheels stuck
in the muddy ruts, is what a boy, a guest
of one of his children, completely unchurched,

muttered when called upon for a verse.
A rolling stone gathers no moss. Jesus!
he cries out, striking his horse, despairing

of the barn, ever putting his harness up,
where *does* it thrive? Heart's-ease,
that flower the blessed call love-in-idleness.

in memory of George Knox (1852-1912)

Trained, Wild or Translucent

1.

Beside the tangled leaves and bud, the thorn.
An angry voice arguing. My father
insisting I'm wrong over and over.
What's the use any more of objecting?
From elsewhere, beyond the medieval stone,
the ribbed vaults, flying buttress and spires
that come to mind as his voice gets louder,
I hear *disappear*, and I am I am
still trying to become invisible,
though, increasingly, what's keeping me here,
what seems insurmountable, I hold dear
as the walls of the Gothic cathedrals
my father, the architect, loves. What's beautiful,
I would learn from him, is always well built.

2.

It was difficult learning from him what was well built. A sad mortar, my stammering he'd interrupt to prove I couldn't possibly mean what I said. At dinner Webster's stood guard at the table, next to his plate. Inside, in those pages, he'd argue meanings were fixed, knots that someone couldn't untie. Couldn't. Could not. I couldn't have said then what I wanted to find—a language to hide in.

3.

Where you find yourself he too is hidden.
Who speaking? I ask, even though I think
it's my voice. Then another's. Much more like
my mother's. Silence. Then *here* at the crossing
where, through the windows in two directions,
blue light is spreading, a wash of rose pink.
Dear, trust in your stillness, let yourself sink
down into it to see how the columns
are bending. Now lean, rest up against them.
Then look as far as you can to the west
where late afternoon sun illuminates
the tracery's stone, every intricate
interlaced branch and trefoil filled with glass.
Yes, stained. And wrought like us all, don't forget.

4.

Overwrought is more like it. How could I forget how I nearly
stopped speaking? In the house my father designed, a clock
chimes. Another time. When I'm young. Back in my room at the
end of the hall. If he knocked then, the door wouldn't open. If
only the girl could escape what is holding her there as Notre
Dame de la Belle Verrière, framed by spirits, a dove haunting her
crown, child in the opaline folds of her gown, will break through
her silence, the glass she's in, with her eyes, say, I am ready to listen.

5.

Though her eyes say, I'm ready to listen,
words fail me as always when asked for. Thrust
and counter-thrust. My own flying buttress,
walls, piers and vaults, a well-designed system
to keep whatever dares to move from moving.
Was it, confess now, a matter of *must*?
All the time thinking no, but saying yes.
Supporting every idea with reasons,
every last feeling. Oh, thin, thin, the wall
may be too thin to bear the weight from above.
But the self, she says now, is more than stone
and translucent, bubble-filled, roughly blown
glass. All this talk without mentioning love—
go find your father in the cathedral.

6.

I find my father in the cathedral
alone at the base of a gentle stair.
How stubborn the mind is, secretive, tiered.
At its darkest, descending, infernal.
But this flight going up, rising at Wells,
these so-called Heavenly Stairs could be breakers
I am watching from a shore far from here.
Admit that the heart, being tender, swells
to enclose the man who fixes the eye
of his camera on the beautiful
light at the top of each step we would call
the crest if truly a wave. I'd ask why
he keeps changing lenses and apertures,
but I understand, being his daughter.

7.

I can understand, being his daughter, how alone in a cathedral this
man who steadies his tripod isn't lonely. More at home within the
hush of damp walls where he will draw, but not pray. Meanwhile,
my mother, knowing she can't disturb him for hours, enters the
garden where heart's-ease, that wild pansy, blooms in the close.
The earliest rose. When I find her she's befriending a stranger.
Reaching out, this is my mother's art. I know, loving her, I resem-
ble my father.

8.

She's here again. Saying how like your father
you are as you write, apart from the rest.
This gloom you're in reveals only the dust
coming down. You notice it flows over
every small thing. But look up, look higher
to see what's been lit by an architect
whose clerestory can bring back the perfect
hours you tend to forget. The summers
in water and woods, trees against the light
that, returning, makes light of everything,
what you, through your own dark, are carrying.
Gothic stone levitates, gravity gone
in this light in which, *listen*, the quiet,
all human longing, yields to evensong.

9.

All human longing yields to evensong
between the altar and crossing. The choir
is filling with voices that will capture
the lengthening shadows, the slow turning
of day into dusk. But now the organ,
countering, questioning, leads them higher
and higher, *here* and *elsewhere*, they answer,
oh, keep it from ending, begin again.
I've never heard men sing so like women.
When the service is over, I remain
in the church with the unseen organist
who, improvising, plays with the passion
of someone who is his own exorcist.
His art, what is released. If not contained.

10.

In art, what is released or contained, I want to say to my father, is
what we fear most—look with me into the corners, at carved cor-
bel and boss, where forms disfigured by terror seem veined with
their makers' nightmares and ours. When anger contorts your face,
I would say, confused by your rage, the cause of your pain, I see
medieval knots of fang and wing, some serpent-men, their scales
entangled, feeding upon themselves. What if no one is free of
grotesquerie, tail, talon or hoof, if this makes us human, what after
all can it mean, this dream?

11.

Father, do you know what it means, this dream
I'm having of you and me in a mote-
filled sanctuary where everything floats,
the prayers and notes (this way, now back)? Even
these, my poor words, seen apart from us, seem
to drift, anchorless. Who knows where I'll go?
Above the door I could open, the rose
that crowns the nave that artisans made gleams,
twined with the climbing rose blooming in time.
Trained, wild or translucent. Will any form
be the one to lead me all the way
there, back to the garden I started from?
A garden? Is this what you mean, you say,
this tangle of blossom and leaf and thorn?

The Knot Garden

The Knot Garden

If she had the time,
if she wasn't always solving a problem

or hemming herself in getting someone
out of a fix,

she'd start out on paper,
sketching first the square, the necessary

enclosure. Then diagonal lines
from opposite corners.

From the center point she'd call "A"
(where the lines crossed)

she'd stretch a string, then rotate it
to draw a circle, this is how she'd begin,

then stop—so many shapes to choose from,
variations on true lovers,

the overhand noose and carrick bend.
Remember the wind knots said to work wonders

for sailors becalmed at sea—untie one
for a good wind, call up a half-gale

with two. But beware of the hurricane,
knots in the wrong hands

she'd think as she cleared the ground,
smoothing the soil on which she would lay

her borders of stone, then weave
with powdered lime Nostalgia for Paradise,

if not Don't Think Twice
or Her Sweet Milk, Heart's-ease.

She'd nearly settled on a name.
But there remained the problem

of cuttings. Which ones? Thrift,
that everlasting green, drew snails.

The hyssop's stalks grew thick. Germander
ran rampant. Under snow, lavender cotton would rot.

So it would be dwarf box,
that slow grower, and intersecting it,

for one plant must overtake its neighbor,
blue mist, maybe blood leaf.

Lastly, inside the strands she'd be shearing
forever (*no loose ends, nothing allowed to unravel*)

which flowers? Perennials? Annuals?
Primrose or daisy? Perhaps the Madonna lily,

the red Martagon. She'd allow herself color
in the loops and the ovals;

after all, what she meant was to make
of the tangled something beautiful—

that's what she'd tell anyone
asking about her garden—

she wanted the kind of knot
the Elizabethans also called a conceit.

No pride in that.

Whatever had she been thinking?

From the beginning. Children. Loving.

She'd made strapwork
of everything.

Florescence

Not to be confused with *fluorescence*,

though most of us know flowers
that seem to emit their own light—

the hot orange stars of the tiger lily.
Or the dogwood,
filling with creamy blooms:

                    a child's globe
when shaken: snow.

Even the blue flame of the iris.
In its depths, the ashes of another world.

Words, the names for things we should remember

and people, too,
at times they trade places

as they did for the man who called his first wife
when the child of his second marriage was born.

Rushing from the delivery room
to the nearest phone, the first call he makes
he makes to her:
                It's a boy.
And for the oddest moment it is theirs,

for what's imprinted within are the births
of his other children,

and with this one call
he brings the woman who left him
back into the room in which they labored together,

their first son so turned in the womb he wouldn't descend
into the polar glare without forceps

and a physician who'd never had a child of her own
but who understood, she said, a woman's pain.

How the man loves himself endlessly,
the woman would think later on,

how he stamps the soft metal
of every experience with his own image,
unchanged over the years.

And she, thin enough to be a single taper,
but burning like a candelabrum—
                              shedding light for everyone—
perhaps she didn't love herself enough,

but I'm no more sure of this
than I am of the cousins of Queen Anne's Lace.
Put me down in damp meadows
and I can't tell the pretty umbrellas apart—

the tiny white flowers of parsnip
looking so like poison hemlock.
                         One medicinal.
The common name of the other
like some awful secret wish that man might have had
all his life: *Mother die.*

When she put the phone down she wondered
how long she could go on hating him.

Sometimes it becomes such a blur,
one feeling overlapping another,
the fields,

         whether we notice or not,
flowering.

Late Summer, Cicadas

Their pitch is the fire
friction makes of brittle kindling,

the preacher again
praising the spirit
risen from the body
crumpled in the back of a pickup.

No blame for the drunk
at the wheel, why grieve?
God has taken Tom from us
so you, his friends,
might be saved.

        *

Buzz, it's all buzz,
the cicada's hoax

or at dusk, another octave
of yearning.

And my son, hearing nothing
but the white noise
of his grief in that summer's heat,
turned away from us all,
leaving the preacher
in his church demanding the saved
raise their hands.

        *

That long season under ground,
how do they climb?
Spiraling upward,
or side to side, sweeping
the interminable dirt?

Leaf, catching an updraft,
then sinking down.

This is the worry
love has become.

Nights a mother lies awake
driven crazy by what sounds like a party
in the trees—insects, siren and infant cry,
a helicopter winging
toward emergency.

                    *

Sleep, sleep, August child
nothing could calm.

One week, the next,
another summer is gone.
By Labor Day, next to the translucent husks
they shed on our porch rail and sill,
the summer bodies
of cicadas end on their backs.
We visit Tom's grave.

I despair of metaphor—
cricket, bird note, how in this poem
even the mother begs to become
an emblem, along with her son,

48

but what else can quiet the racket
loud as a cicada makes
from the delicate membranes
close to its heart?

The Prodigal's Mother Speaks to God

When he returned a second time,
the straps of his sandals broken,
his robe stained with wine,

it was not as easy to forgive.

By then his father
was long gone himself,

leaving me with my other son, the sullen one
whose anger is the instrument he tunes
from good morning on.

I know.

There's no room for a man
in the womb.

But when I saw my youngest coming from far off,
so small he seemed, a kid
unsteady on its legs.

She-goat
what will you do? I thought,
remembering when he learned to walk.

Shape shifter! It's like looking through water—
the heat bends, it blurs everything: brush, precipice.

A shambles between us.

The Seed of Her Name

John 8:1-11

She worked the flax with her hands
while her mind, that wanderer, led elsewhere,

following the village's women
down the vineyard slope to the spring,

following without hearing
what they who shunned her were whispering

as they herded their children ahead of them.
Returning to the distaff

she spins the rest:
if you only knew, they say,

the merchants who cheat them
the mothers-in-law in their homes,

even husbands—
pits to spit out.

Then as easily as from the rosy, the pale flowering
of the sesame, the seed of her own name

falls next, and the women descend altogether,
peck at what's dropped.

Meanwhile from her doorway
she sees the children tiring of other games

start to toss a rotting lemon
back and forth, all laughter

until one gets hit, in anger throws
the first stone,

and green as in the earliest pressing,
the oil of the unripened olive on the tongue,

a cry from one of their own
causes the mothers to rise

suddenly, make of themselves
a gritty, stinging desert

wind—an inscription even she,
illiterate and barren, understands:

a woman will turn on anyone
but her children.

Ruined

That night a stranger walking down the road
would take her for a woman weeding late—
that's all, she thought, all, all the time
I'm breaking, can't anyone hear my heart?
At that, she snapped a plant off stem and bud
to fling away. Another. Pepper, stalks
of corn. Raked spinach out in handfuls. Crushed
it underfoot. What when the sun rose would
he say to the ruin? Couldn't know—alone—
far from here by morning—she could only
imagine the look she'd carry like a cameo
inside. Opening to his face long after
this night. She'd leave her lover a keepsake, too,
a tale to tell to bookish friends of his.
A version, they'll think, of one they've known
all along. This garden he'd remember her by.

Memorial

They elude us
like the beauty
who turned away from the artist:

her plum-dark hair
the length of the kimono
she's wearing

having fallen as water does over rock
to pool quietly near the hem.
The bluish-black of the damson—

her treasure—combed over silk:
all together, a burnished plumage,
gold folding over olive

over royal blue to the end.
The brightest threads
so like the flush that surprises us

inside the plum—part sour,
part something else.
Why think of sadness?

We're swimming now
midst a suite of feathery fins,
and if she turned toward us

what would we see beneath the swift currents
of her eyes, fathoms down?
Though we'd have her an empress,

it's likely she's just one of a host
arriving by accident,
at risk of vanishing

without the artist.
And so our departed
brushes, brushes us.

From the Sketchbooks of Vanessa Bell

Self-Portrait of the Artist

I am wading through masses of currants,
stripping them into bottles,
six done, three more now,

and the bushes are laden. English red,
goya, blood underlying vermilion.
A painter starting over

scrapes off layer after layer.
How small the berry becomes
under the knife, how still.

Inside, near the tart center,
where the eye is a liar,
the tongue remembers.

It's a shudder of mind
that seizes the globe,
swallows it whole.

Study for an Interior With the Artist, Leslie Stephen and Virginia Woolf

It was never easy
being Virginia Woolf's sister.
When we were young,

Father's favorite, she'd hide
outside of his study, keeping her distance
while, inside, he raved at me.

Though she could see through the door standing open
how, as skillfully as the best models at the Academy,
I did not blink, did not stretch a limb,

she couldn't have known how much I missed Mother,
dead then two years, how alone without her,
the eighteen-year-old mistress of the house,

I feared the inquisition those Wednesdays
Father checked my accounts,
weeks I was ten, eleven pounds over.

No one knew
how by picturing a scene
I learned I could leave it.

I am drawing Vanessa still,
now, as then, determined not to alter a feature
in my rendering,

the arms ending at her waist
in one quiet fist.
Eyes marooned in that resolute face,

she could be at sea, so far
is she from her father,
who, in his rocking, gets smaller

and smaller, his voice fading away
until it makes no difference if his mouth still moves,
she no longer hears what he's saying.

Study for "Adam and Eve," 1913

She was never far from us,
floating spirit
at the edge of a scene,

flame in the Florentine evening.
May, 1909—
Virginia, asleep in England.

My husband and I after dinner
on the verandah of our hotel,
32, Via Romana.

Imagine a woman
admiring the forms and fading colours
of olive and grape distant from London's scrim,

the man who seeing in his wife
her sister's face
reaches for her hand. *She*

is in his fingers, on his breath,
the woman thinks. And now the firefly
in the grass dazzles them both.

When the chapter ended,
we were all expelled from the garden.
I, who cannot speak of my pain,

Virginia, always wishing to be forgiven,
and Clive, who learned from her
the words to betray me.

The Artist in Her Studio

Finally alone, without daughter
or sons, my brush the only tongue moving.
Curves and hollows,

deep shadows and silver edges.
In the quiet, even the tiresome coal scuttle
assumes a secret life.

Sometimes, beneath the touchable surface,
mine reveals itself, cobalt blue
beneath the body's apparent blush,

interlocking circles, intersecting lines.
It's a particular window, north light,
everyone else is sleeping.

Look and look
and you can leave the material world
for a vanishing point.

Study for "Interior With Two Women," 1932

When she wrote *Orlando*
my sister imagined a single life
in which one could be a man

and also a woman.
I have never imagined myself
like that. But I know the tissue-thin division.

Shoreline. The least wind altering the fringe.
The indeterminate hours, dusk
and, sometimes, if we're lucky,

the awakening.
Where there was one woman,
there are two when I step back,

put down my pencil,
pick it up. The seated figure in sleeves
seems about to smooth the pleats in her skirt

while opposite
the nude covers the place
where her sex folds in on itself.

What would they say to one another
if they could speak, for once
more than oil and dust,

the slippery medium
that quiets the whispering in the hedge,
the secrets the garden would tell,

except for this.
I will paint the coal stove
dead center in the canvas

like the vertical support
for a balance.
Breast for bodice, lit face

counterweight for the dark,
the beam levels: this is my balm,
my art.

Untitled Drawing

Shrapnel. That light
blinds fail to shut out.
I cannot bear to see.

When I open my eyes, my son's chest
opens. Closing them
changes nothing.

What has art to do with this, Velázquez?
I cannot even begin—
every way an impasse

between the Prado and the grave
where his beloved Republicans
buried my Julian.

Landscape in Wartime, May 1941

I imagine it's like blackout driving.
All the landscapes one has known,
the margins of the road obscured.

A kind of fog.
And for those the loved one's left behind?
For them as well the road goes on and on—

one cannot recognize a thing.
The windows with their blackout curtains
drawn, brick like stone, colour gone

and over all of this—the gloom,
the lamps that one has navigated by
put out—the Germans fly unseen.

Madness. The way they'd invade Sussex.
The static of guns. Nothing
intelligible. Broken syllables,

then something
like the current
that carried my sister away.

Self-Portrait: 30 May 1944

All night, powered by a dynamo
that thunders away in a nearby field,
a searchlight scans the sky for the enemy,

and I, turning over the drawings
I've made through the years,
look into these mirrors

for some other shape the light might return to me,
nothing the soldiers camped close to us
could see, no, in the still field

of my house, this room
I would fill the frame like the giant moth
I remember against our pane.

As large as a bat, bird, nothing
could kill it—not even chloroform.
The moth took its own slow time.

Landscape, Virginia's House

Today the light is irresolute,
pastel rising over the hills,
levitating in the mist,

then settling down over the tomatoes
and onions, the kitchen garden.
I follow it across the yard

as it skims the water lilies
in the pond, the columbine,
to the great elm

where Virginia's ashes lie.
I am less interested these days
in how we fell away from each other.

The light that dusts the surface,
sticks and the grey-blue stones water burnishes,
flowing over everything, may be perfect,

though what it glazes is flawed. Love,
love seems lately
to abide in the light.

Ruined Frescoes, 1949

Here now in Pisa I imagine the stench
on that blistering day,
German, American bombers over the city,

the lead roof of the Campo Santo
melting down over its walls, ruining
all those beautiful frescoes.

Incendiary heart,
when will the burning stop?
What can appease it?

Surely not a birthmark or breast,
a child's braided hair—
the whole panicked town

at best a blur from the cockpit
as Giotto's vision, holy mother
and son, darkened and ran.

What remains? The rubble of Pisa,
my firstborn dead, I am thinking
on the long walk from the station.

And then, to find what the war revealed
under the plaster applied bit by bit
as if beneath consciousness,

deep as earliest sight:
the elaborately human studies of saints,
drawn in the freest hand.

Our semblance,
what is finally
unfinished.

Study for a Portrait of Virginia Woolf

I will paint her one last time,
not from life as then,
1912, my easel propped upon the lawn,

Virginia still young
in a wide-brimmed hat,
head tilted back,

after her long flirtation
with Clive. Four years—between us
the rope that was my husband.

Listen.
A child is crying
from another part of the garden,

a stray gull seeking its bearings. This
and the postman knocking,
the cows at milking, a distant hammering,

all of it, the din
of conscience. But no apology,
no confession.

Half hidden by my easel,
I pressed my brush against her nose and mouth
till she could neither breathe

nor see—losing face that time
literally. To finish her
I knotted red about her neck;

choosing brown for her last dress
I lay her out—
the only way I had of saying how I felt.

Now I imagine her begging for her life:
Nessa, what were those four years
against the forty since? she asks.

After everything, Sweet William,
her namesake, blooms this spring, floating pink
above the lawn's green rim,

the porcelain
I place the clusters in to paint
again. A flower in water,

the face I catch now in my studio mirror
seems for a moment her own.
Full Stephen mouth, eyes the grey-blue

of pebbles along my garden's path,
or darker, where they lie unsettled,
buried in the River Ouse. Water by bending the light

so blurs the here and now with before
I turn from my palette.
Her last portrait will be a silhouette,

for my hand remembers the outline
of her face as well as an old horse knows
the way home, uphill and down,

where the road curves, gravel turns now
to dust. In the late afternoon sun of Sussex
I am drawing her, in ink this time.

She might call what I'm doing
revision, understanding the light we're in,
like the story, keeps changing.

In the Heartland

Appearance at Dusk

Between midday and midnight,
the scales just so.
Too late for shadows

she disturbed the equilibrium
of dusk so little as she passed,
I doubted the murky air

had moved at all. You know
in water when something stirs up
the bottom, a cloud of sediment rises—

I questioned if anything happened,
and then she was there,
my answer, where the apples had fallen.

I thought as soon as she saw me
she'd turn, she'd disappear,
but she bent to eat

the ripe fruit cast upon the ground,
her white tail wagging
like some domesticated creature

before the deer looked up again.
This time fixing me
with a gaze that left me fallow.

I don't know how she put to rest
everything that eddied within me, how
as long as we kept one another in sight

windfall could have given way
to snowfall beyond us.
Beyond this stillness, the heady branches,

were they banished?
Only to be sent for
when another spring came:

the hard buds; blossoms;
dawn on the new globes of Winesap,
Delicious—summer, summer again

amid the terror, evenings and mornings
when I'd scare, when I would have bolted
if love hadn't held me here.

In the Heartland

The farms go on
like the ocean. To what end?
Winter is one thing,
summer another, but for this color,
call it *march*, richer than dun,
paler than mud, look within.
What's there? Anything growing?
Even the question's gone flat.
So we hold it up—
whatever is nearest. Say *like that*:
the fallen oak leaf. Imagine
acres of them laid stem to stem.
The fine veins and finer,
hairlines even a well-made bowl
retains from its firing.

And between the fields, no hedgerows.
Hems, neatly stitched. Where's
the farmer, the farmer's wife?
Hi-ho, who's left
standing alone? House, barn, silo, house,
the plot repeating itself
demands the artist
take up her brush,
lay down titanium white,
great bars of it, those interstates
running away.

Or is it more as if the teacher's chalk
made them? What *is* the heartland's lesson?
And does it have seasons? What would it be

in the greening of spring?
After a harvest, the blonde stalks leveled?
A pleasure to read
in summer, full of news,
the daily paper

seen now from the air
(*whereto? wherefore?*)
is a blank.
Nothing. Nothing again.
Its dominion.

The Storm

During the storm I think I am dreaming,
silver arc and answering clap,
I am dreaming the wind an ax

that splits the linden in half.
And what? What's within?
An inky disclosure

now I see, yes,
a mass hoarding its ore:
the honey

until now I hadn't imagined
was there, like the manuscript
in a cramped hand

found after a lifetime,
a crowd of sentences
that clarifies everything, the hive swarming,

the villagers who must account
for what they have stolen
or whatever I was thinking

when, so thunderous was it,
a planet cracked along its axis,
the tree on my house

seemed in that blinding moment
to have fallen into the room
where I lay. And the queen

in her ruptured cell,
how long had she been sleeping
that sleep which is a bondage?

She has, she thinks, no memory
of the unshuttered blue she wakes to,
the wing-blur of leavings and comings

about her, the dizzying go-rounds
of her sunny new sphere,
oh, where is she being ferried?

Past pollen, detritus,
gold leaf, fluff, what's next
on the spangled horizon?

On the Prairie

Look down at your feet
    or straight ahead
as you walk
    and you easily miss them,

which is why it took me the longest time to see
    against the backcloth
of a blue June morning
    their fluff, their gauziness.

Fill a horizon with them
    and you'd have a fine haze,
but that can't happen, traveling as they do,
    one by one,

or as a smattering the sun catches
    on their way down,
no more than a dusting.
        The distance between where they begin

and where they land
    no one would call a straight line.
They even look a little woozy,
    wooly-headed,

these web-selves
    just released, giddy with freedom.
I guess they're the aerial seeds
    of the cottonwood tree,

though you have to take this
    on faith—what they were fastened to

I can't see from here.
　　No kiss and tell

for these itinerants,
　　though they teach by example.
And the rest of us,
　　by contrast, illustrate what they aren't:

the smallest of insects, the gnat,
　　a whirligig
next to the cottonwood tuft;
　　flies dodging one another,

nearly colliding, a hurly-burly
　　about to become the whirlwind
I'm usually spinning within—even on a good morning
　　the birds on the prairie

are bombardiers. A sparrow
　　tails a hawk,
a redwing shadows me
　　as I pass the cattails where it hides its nest.

All the while the cotton-creatures sail by,
　　desultory as pollen,
and so like miniature cumuli,
　　looking up now I'm having trouble

distinguishing them
　　from the clouds on an updraft
they're floating toward.
　　I cannot trust my sight.

This has happened before,
　　hasn't it? Is always always

happening. If only I heard a tintinnabulum,
    the smallest tinkling bell

ringing when something's real,
    so I would know;
if I could hold, just for a moment,
    what spirits this close—

but caught,
    and in my damp palm,
what was like unto a breeze,
    what-I-would-be

sticks,
    even when I say *go*,
sally forth, it stays, will not, little soul
    of mine, ghost.

The Barred Owl

His trumpet wakes me nightly
with its reveille of eight short blasts,
each rhyming with the next

before the last note drops—
what worries him so late?
In the dark, the carved face

nowhere to be seen, the trees
on the other side of the glass
dense as a medieval tapestry's,

how can I tell?
Falling back into the sleep
the owl roused me from,

I dream the hunt,
spears, the river a stag must cross.
Everywhere small birds and rodents

an owl, come hunger, may prey upon.
Who looks for you,
who looks for you all?

Maybe this is the question the barred owl asks—
we hear what we want to hear, don't we?
The way until I saw its name in a book

I thought the barred owl
bard. And even now, acknowledging
the markings, the dark cross-barring,

I listen for what a poem provides:
that moment when question
and answer blur, hunter

and hunted are stilled.
Stopped in their tracks, they catch their breath
in the silk and wool of their surroundings,

a weft of sweet violets.
It might as well be woven
for all time: the hounds resting,

the weary drinking their fill from the spring.
In the heart of the woods,
an owl, beyond harm, looking on.

After Ovid

I kneeled, I lay down
next to it, and still no fish,
no frog or insect surfaced.

No mayfly, stonefly,
dragon or damsel
beginning in water

as nymph. In the heart
of a prairie, in a pool
barely the depth of my hand

the sand at the bottom
spun round and around
drawing me down

as if toward the source of churning
in the world of trembling aspen,
hawkweed and stargrass,

each on the edge of becoming
something else—
the voice

I heard then from the water
weeping as a mother does for her child,
one in grief so long I'd swear

her limbs had thinned to splinters,
the bow of one arm and the other's arrow
whittled so, she could no longer aim.

Fortress-back, the hills of her shoulders, pelvic sling,
all relented. Even what had been soft
to begin with, belly and breasts,

gave in. Kin of wind,
what she'd been goddess of
she became.

Afterward

Amid the debris,
the wreckage of events,
it was somehow as unbroken
in its way
as the egg found in the rubble
of a leveled house
or, under the dust
that was someone's good china
once, the teacup
rimmed in gold leaf,
a baby unearthed
alive, or, most surprising perhaps,
in working order
the chimes of the quarter hour
a man heard standing atop a staircase
leading nowhere:
amid the debris, a little melody
rung against something bigger,
louder, the megaphone of the twister,
the line she would sing to herself.

The Whooping Cranes

Perhaps it began with a disturbance
hardly worth mentioning,
or something larger, some hurt we need to name,

having felt endangered
as—shy, secretive—
the whooping cranes have been.

Farmers, hunters, high power lines.

Of the hundreds once: a few dozen cranes.
And those remaining have forgotten their way

so that—who would believe?—to save them,
a man dresses up in a crane costume,
his head, face, the rest swaddled in white cotton.

Not unlike us, the way writers pretend,

the biologist starting in the bulrushes
with the olive-buff eggs he'll protect,

later helping the chicks find minnows and snails,
frogs and larvas to grow on,
this man who has not begotten them,

but father-like leads the fledglings around the refuge,
their plumage whitening
against the black muck of the marsh

before they follow him into the sky

to ride the wing of the ultra-light aircraft
he pilots, glide behind.

And while they're aloft
the man who looks like he's towing the flock
confuses himself with the cranes—
as they do themselves with him—

their cries in his throat,
his costume, down-soft,
nothing his own but blue eyes showing.

Under a spell as he flies,
he remembers the story
of the seven ravens he loved as a child—

how anger, one burst from their father,
turned the sons into birds.

Lifting off in an early mist he wonders
if he'd want in the end
the gift their sister brings to the glass mountain,

unsure if freedom lies in becoming human.

How well he knows
it's only the beginning of a long migration—

a thousand miles
starting from Wisconsin's wetlands, stopping
for high winds and hail, then on in formation
over ponds, swales and grasslands, the ridges of Appalachia

to where, if they arrive, the flock will winter over
in the southern haven of a salt marsh
and, come spring, fly back without him, wild.

In Midair

She would drink on the wing,
planing the surface of a pond
just long enough to swallow once.

Hunger, too,
would seem a gloss, marginalia
whatever wants she'd had before.

She would fly as far as Saturn
and never land, unbanded,
no one's courier, no one calling her home

she'd fly like a grace note,
little else, she'd embellish herself,
ghosting catch-as-catch

can. Even sleeping,
the occasional flicker of a wing
to keep her aloft

would feel nothing like treading
to stay afloat,
fearful as she'd been of drowning.

Love, too, would be aerial
then—a shallow glide, a swift darning
as easily undone,

and free falling, she'd know
the windblown net of this afterlife
stretched out beneath her.

Mount Joy

If we live *uphill*
from the Mount Joy Baptist Church

what heights of happiness have we reached?
But before we get carried away,

let's not forget this is the Midwest,
where elevation is measured

by how far the river's risen
this year, how many farms have gone under.

Here, where the only angels
are an attending mongrel and the wingless deer,

we're putting in tomatoes,
putting what faith we have in Miracle-Gro

while the worshipers gather below us,
early service and late, their cars

crowding the shoulders of Schwartz Street.
What, pray, is our gospel?

In what tongue our raspberry tangle,
overgrown lilies, the dill seeds in furrows?

We are still talking of last year's cankered fruit,
asking what part water, how much nitrogen

feeds the blossom
when we're brushed by a single brindled wing. *Hallelujah!*

he'd exclaim, if he could,
this dog of ours, ecstatic from chasing rabbits

and squirrels to the creek.
As unmusical as he in this incarnation,

we've stopped working
and are listening now as we lean on our shovels,

for it's carrying up the hill, over
the potholes, the pitted road,

toward our garden,
where we hear the Baptists singing of heaven.

The Deer

What the deer at night consume
may be what we thought we needed
but can live without.

Try to forget your labor, the hours
you dug out the grove of young walnuts
to fill the neglected arbor with sun—

the vines like someone's handwriting
gone haywire with age,
wandering outside the lines.

Watching as you re-strung
what was left years ago to die,
I doubted anything could bloom,

but soon enough, tendrils, leaves,
then pea-sized grapes bubbled up,
chameleon-green clusters.

And as quickly as one can read
into the smallest gesture
the future, we conjured the mussel-blue

Concord—then, just as fast,
because the past is nobody's fool,
the sweet skin of someone gone.

We each have our own aftertaste
(in the vines, the bees tracing figure eights),
what our years of plenty rub up:

a flurry of talcum, a scented wrist.
Then (worse?)—remembering how to shine
the grape as if wiping a film of dust

from a picture of what was once.
A vintage.
And those who tended us.

And the deer, what memories
lodged in their bodies,
what hunger, as they helped themselves

to our unripe fruit? Under the poor lantern
of the moon, stealthy ghosts,
they stripped the grapes

as we slept, dreaming as always
our versions of Pharaoh's dream.
We could grieve awake,

but given the liquid passage of the animal
through the dark, a current,
like it or not, we can't stop,

we go out after dinner to watch
the doe and her young feed on our apples.
Beautiful thieves, in the falling light

the color of grain
the wise store inside
after the growing season is over.

Allison Funk is the author of two earlier collections of poems, including *Living at the Epicenter*, which won the Samuel French Morse Prize. Other honors include a fellowship from the National Endowment for the Arts, the George Kent Prize from *Poetry*, and the Celia B. Wagner Prize from the Poetry Society of America. Her poems have appeared in *Poetry*, *The Paris Review*, *Shenandoah*, *The Georgia Review*, and other journals. She is Professor of English at Southern Illinois University at Edwardsville.